INFINITY BROKEN AND NOT

AND NOT

FINDING A PLACE AMONG THE PARTICLES

STEPHANIE DOWLING

Copyright © 2021 Stephanie Dowling

All rights reserved. No portion of the book may be reproduced or utilized in any form or by any means, electronic or mechanical, including photocopying, recording, or by any other information storage and retrieval system, without permission in writing from the author.

Book layout: www.bookclaw.com

FOREWARD

I have followed Stephanie's writings for years & so happily applaud her compiling them for publication. As I read each (over & over) I think of the many clients, elders & youth I'd love to share these with. Surely they, and anyone who sits with Stephanie's words & images, will see their reflection.

Yet, more than resonating with pieces, gathered together under: First Part, Next Part, Which Part, Last Part, readers will be coaxed to dive into the "so much more" waiting to be discovered.

Stephanie writes of the universal pilgrimage to the center of one's Self. And with each advance along the way, she reassures, encourages and dares readers to trust their hesitant steps and pace. As in her piece on Shadow: "She was simply the messenger. And I am who I am because she kept on coming. Now I even welcome her, because good God, look at those eyes. She loves me."

Stephanie speaks to that which comes before thought, which arises through whispers of instinct, dreams or musings of the soul. She brings them to the page and one can't help but accept the invitation to stay, allow and discover. With everyday language she delicately captures edges of expression to honor their fullness and their contradiction. As in Light Interrupted "It was lonely in the light at first." And in No: "It will save your soul & hand you a life, This wonderful, little Two-letter Word."

Grace, freedom, courage, permission and hard won wisdom guide the reader to remember & embody what is theirs. And to proclaim what is not. Through highlighting & honoring all the dimensions of one's unfolding self, Stephanie ignites a willingness & conviction to go on. And to trust in whatever awaits; in the stillness, the shadows and the light.

Jane M. Hart, Ed.D.

INTRODUCTION

INFINITY BROKEN AND NOT is a developmental journey through psychological and spiritual growth, via humanistic poetry. I wrote this book because the gifts I've been given throughout my lifetime do not belong to me - they are to be shared and passed around. They have saved me and helped me to grow. These words are for human beings who are wanting and needing to be seen as they curse, contemplate, wonder about and search for a place among the particles.

This book is a mirror, a push, and a hug. It is acceptance, directions, and love.

TABLE OF CONTENTS

FIRST PART 1
    While I Was Here 2
    response-ability 3
    A Question of Worth 4
    Find A Way 5
    I've Got You 6
    This Darkness 7
    Ride 8
    Shadow 9
    make room. 10
    Enough 11
    decide 12
    Stillness 13
    Where There Is Light 14
    Round & Round 15
    Fire Wire Fuse 16
    manifest 17
    Swirl 18
    Clean Generosity 19
    Fly 20
    Negotiation 21

NEXT PART 25
    Drive 26
    Choose 27
    Gently 28
    Practice 29
    Directions 30
    Perfectionism 31
    Green Eyed 32
    Time & Futility 33

Whispers 34
validation 35
Moving On 36
Go 37
vigilance 38
Ancestors 39
double god bless 40
It Hurts 41
integrity 42
Light Interrupted 43
jive 44
Let It Pour 45

WHICH PART **49**
Stones 50
freedom 51
Emotional Currency 52
Slay 53
No 54
The Wolves 55
most things 56
Begin Again 57
Swing 58
Within 59
magic 60
Honor 61
honor is a verb 62
Absolutely 63
Allow It 64
Arranging Furniture 65
the Tao 66
Inside Out 67
loved 68
In Further 69

LAST PART 73
   Silly 74
   Truth & Tea 75
   Humility 76
   I miss her 77
   Unfurl 78
   wise & beautiful 79
   Unzippable Skins 80
   Sublime 81
   The Need 82
   free 83
   Well – Worn 84
   Perspective 85
   I Am You 86
   I Am New 87
   Goals 88
   Infinity Broken 89
   Risk 90
   Dear Past Self 91
   Dig 92
   no more 93

FIRST PART

While I Was Here

While I was here, assisted by many, I learned to walk a path
that seemed unbearable, unjust & cruel.

Gifted a willingness to not only survive, but to thrive,
I asked for the courage to do the very scary things...

I began to tell the truth and live in the light.
I began to forge a path born of my Soul.

I began to thrive on courage and I began to feed on truth.

Then I watched as the path circled back on itself,
casting a spell of response-Ability.

So, with courage & willingness and honor & gratitude...
I assisted others while I was here.

response-ability
changes everything

A Question of Worth

I used to wonder about my worth, big time.

Then, someone else outside of me challenged my worth.
(my usefulness, my intelligence, my fortitude, my integrity, my relevance)

I had to dig deep and answer for myself, and by myself,
if I embodied those qualities or not.

...Turns out...I did & I do - in all aspects.

And then I wondered if I needed to be all of those things,
all the time, to be worth "it".
(someone else's time, respect, consideration)

...Turns out...No - I don't.

Now it's about me & only me,
and it's not about me at all.
It's about:

Is it
(connection, communion, intimacy with my god, my goodness, my highest self)

"worth it"
(the effort, the risk, the vulnerability, the time, the energy)

?

...Turns out...Yes.
Yes, it is.

Every. Single. Time.

Find A Way

It occurs to me now, in the dark & in the quiet, that the gifts that I got from my mom are the exact things I needed...

to save myself from the things that she, herself,
could not save herself,
or me,
from.

It's a wild whirlwind of a ride
to find a way to the light,
when the way in is through
the darkness & shadows & fog.

May the walk for you,
turn into a hopeful, knowing
jog.

I've Got You

Should you find yourself in the hallway
between one door that has closed
while searching for one that is open,
notice the flux
between grounded, centered & calm,
and complete & total panic.

Remember to be patient and to trust.
Float around in the grace
of your timely preparation...

for now,
for this next level,
for what is finding its way toward you.

Sit still.
Listen to your Self
tell yourself,

"I've got you."

This Darkness

Breathwork opened some door - some hole in the floor - some eye in the sky, that could see me. It chose me - to no longer be ridden by the madness - but to ride it.

It looked like - felt like - smelled like R-A-G-E.

It consumed me - until I became it - some wild, open throated beast - roaring from the center - veins popping - eyes bulging out of my head.

It took hold of my limbs - fists clenched - claws sprawled and wide - wanting - needing to rip and tear - until I collapsed - into a weeping pile of weakness and wanting - "Mommy."

Whimpering for relief - no understanding - a warm wash of tears - into the darkness - music blasting - help me with knowing.

Please. What is happening?

And then there was this:
"Ride".

Ride the dark horse.
With grace and pride, ride.

It is different each time -

the hollows -
the moonlight, stabbing through the leaves -
ducking under branches - eating shadows - hitting trees.

Yet, this is what you came for - this is yours to do.

Take it. Transform it.
This darkness belongs to you.

Ride

When a day feels like a week,
and a week feels like a day,

and all you can do
is ride the ride,

then ride.

Surrender &
breathe &
ride.

Shadow

I used to get blind-sided - flattened - trampled - emptied of all that I was - out of nowhere, by the simplest of things. And somehow, I got up again & again - confused, weary, tired.

After a while, I could see it coming from off in the distance - my shadow. It would thunder toward me & knock me over. It would throw me down on the floor. I mostly landed on my ass, on my head, or on my own broken heart.

I tried to deny its existence. I tried to dodge & weave. I hid behind things that essentially caused me even more harm. My efforts were of no use. She continued to find me.

A few times, in a complete rage, I grabbed her by the mane. I jumped on her back. I rode her & I made her work for me.
My false feelings of triumph were only ever - fleeting.

Finally, I stood still. I surrendered. I listened with my whole Self.
It was then that I remembered, or was reminded...

Every single thought, word, deed & emotion, every touch, taste, sight & sound has a memory.
Each of these seek to be honored in some way.

She was simply the messenger.
And I am who I am because she kept on coming.

Now I even welcome her, because good God,
look at those eyes.
She loves me.

"walk with me.
make room for me.
spend some time with me,"
her shadow said.

"for I come,
bearing your greatest gifts."

Enough

Cross the line and step into a brand-new paradigm.
"Enough" is not an amount - it's a decision.

We decide our own worth, our own value.
We decide the direction of our own life energy.

We can decide to stop leaking it, like a holey oil pan,
leaving a trail of dirty need everywhere we go.

Mental constructs can be daunting & painful & fragile like that.

Rusty old cages are no match for simple clarity
and conscious choosing.

May we demonstrate deciding like our hair is on fire,
so that others may be guided
by that light.

enough
is not an amount
it's a decision

Stillness

Watch all day as the waves come in.

They come in & roll out,
come in & roll out
like breath, but much slower.

Fear
Anger
Sadness
Hope

Fear
Anger
Sadness
Hope

Relax into each.

Let them come.
Let them go.

Wait.

Be still.
- watching -

Be still.
- waiting -

This is no day at the beach.

Where There Is Light

When I feel lost, I get quiet.

I ask.
I listen.
I imagine.
I dream.
I write.
I wait.

I trust that my life energy will not be wasted.
It simply needs some time to find its way...

its passion - its wanting - its delight - its desire.
That is where there is Light.
That is the direction that I take.

I begin to walk.
One step at a time.
One concrete action at a time.

Watching, listening,
feeling my way through

to meet my own
sweet truth.

Round & Round

Life as a human can feel paper thin
- the pages - the phases - the times we feel so wise -
only to find, in another time, how little we knew back then.

When does it stop?

The growing - the learning
- the leveling up - the tearing it down -
the sorting - the keeping - the giving - the chucking
- the right sizing -
again & again...

Could it be that this was what the carousel was for?

To affirm some intrinsic knowing that
we get on - we spin - we get off
and go home?

... always wanting to return - reminiscing - anticipating the ride and the sweetness...
always forgetting the dizziness

... needing some simple freedom and fun...
and to be taken care of by someone

waiting at the exit.

Fire Wire Fuse

When neurons and circumstance hold hands and dance,
they fire, they wire and fuse.
They burn deep grooves, like a hot snake, into your landscape.
They twist their way into your brain, your behavior,
your breath & your bones.

Stay on the planet long enough
to know your map, your mothered mountains, molehills & mines.
Understand where they lead and then choose where to travel.
Watch where you walk and look so, so deeply at the details.
Like a painter in love, capture the contours,
the edges, the shadows, the light.

You can tip toe around on yesterday's tracks,
or pack your own pick, shovel, axe.
Gather all your tools and a team of friends to help you.

Bury the old. Build the new.
Find furrows & forts & fare ways.
Be bouncy or timid, timely or bold.

Bypass the roads that no longer serve you
or get you to whom you want to be.

Participate. Play. Exalt in your existence.

For the earth moves,
as you Do.

what matters
makes matter
manifest mindfully

Swirl

Spend some time in
constructive imagination...

quietly, gently,
without rush or hurry,

build a house
that does not yet exist.

Enjoy the swirl of energy
that calls to the stars
&
tugs at your hair.

Turn
around & around
in seemingly
meaningless circles,

creating a funnel for the heavens
to slide down & land

right where
you are.

Clean Generosity

The lily pad waits - wide open - wondering what you will choose.

Available for anything, while not doing nothing,
she collects the sun, to ignite your soul...
birthing perfect petals,
with disciplined lines & colors,
just to pop you some joy.

Take your time.

Carefully contemplate your way, among the shadows & the light.

Rest your head & gently bob the days away.
Jump from one to the other
like a little kid lost
in the beauty of the moments.

Either way, she is strong enough to hold you.

Open wide and waiting, wondering what you will choose,
available for anything.

Clean generosity.

The lily pad waits.

Fly

Peering out from the protected place of
thinking & planning & wishing & wanting & waiting
but not ever really doing...

Who are we protecting? And what are we protecting them from?
Easily and naturally, like blinking & breathing, the answer sllithers in...

"Me, of course. Myself.
I am protecting my Self
from
rejection & failure, ridicule & flailing,
and from looking stupid & being judged and
from the discomfort of not knowing outcomes."

When I hide & you hide, and they hide & we hide,
the question naturally shifts.

"Why?"

Why do we perpetuate the lie
rather than spread our wings

and fly?

Negotiation

They sat in silence for quite some time,
The Woman & The Little Girl,

the space between them thick and heavy,
as negotiations lingered.

It was anybody's guess, really,
which one would rule the day.

NEXT PART

Drive

My mom used to point at me sometimes, and yell, "You're on my shit list!"
She never told me how I got on there, exactly, or how to get off.

That sucked... her being mad, me being desperate to correct
some elusive, unspecified mistake.

I was little. She was big. She was driving the bus.

When I'm mad now, it's usually at myself.
I walk around confused, wondering,
"What the hell is wrong with me?" and,
"Why can't I get anything right?"

Then I run around, desperately trying to correct
some elusive, unspecified mistake.
Still sucks.

By not paying attention to what's in front of me,
by being driven by Back Then,
I crash into the people I love.

My body grabs my attention.
Neck - shoulders - belly - jaw...
Dull and painful passengers, all.

"Shhh.
Slow down.
Remember that you are big.
Remember that this is your bus and that you know how to drive.
You're a good driver."

I realize that my mom is not actually here anymore.

I take myself off the shit list.
I don't take the ride.
I drive.

**Choose
Choose
Choose**

Consciously & Continuously

Choose

Gently

We are all eternal souls,
newly navigating these tiny, temporary bodies.

Expecting to know
how to drive this thing,
really well, all the time, is simply:

so foolish
so unreasonable
so out of place

that it could be amusing
if it didn't hurt so much.

It's still ridiculous & ludicrous, regardless.

Keep Moving Gently Forward.

Persistence. Action. Attitude. Direction.

May all of us be kind
to our
temporary, resilient, gorgeous,
intelligent, evolving,

perfectly
imperfect
selves.

**practice
instant
forgiveness**

Directions

Today, so far, this Body has experienced:

some wind on its skin, some sunshine too, warm sweet coffee going down smooth, morning bird song, wicker beneath an arm, and a soft, soft pillow under the butt butt.

The thoughts of the Mind
That have drifted by,
include things like:

- expectations for self and others -
- judgement of self -
- judgement of others -

- concern for self and others -
- gratitude & acceptance for self and others -

and then, some amusement
at the humanity of
Thoughts.

But these are all container-y type things.

I practice putting eyes
inside the inside.

I like to say an earnest "Hello!" & "Thank you."
to my wise, old Soul.

And then, for manner's sake, and not too quickly,
I look for a way to ask directions.

Perfectionism

Perfectionism.
You. Fuck.

Cloaked in judgement, heart of stone,
you silently sow lies,
and whispers of safety
through your pet,
Procrastination.

"Tomorrow - tomorrow - tomorrow,"
biding your time to dig out dark spaces,
where fear & shame can do your dirty.

weighting
weighting
weighting
the wings
of those whose only wish
is to help another fly.

You reap paralysis upon your victims,
as they turn your hateful eyes inward on themselves,
assuming your cloak.

You choke out poetry, art, music,
movement
- forever frozen -
never to feel the simple glory
of sunshine & wind
on their tender skin.

Playing with you is a losing game.

I hereby refuse your entry
by making a massive mess of things,
loudly & often.

I shall smile as you scream,
taking note & painting pictures,

while you dissolve in despair
at my joy.

Green Eyed

Jealous of them, I dishonor me
&
my journey, my path,
my work, my fight,
my gifts, my true loves
...my light.

How dare I not stand tall in me,
after all that I have lived through & lost,
walked through & learned from,
seen & survived,
left behind, picked up, cleaned up, integrated
and have offered up to others?

In the flash of one green eye, I was free.

In one quick moment of connecting my heart
to my own life,
I unlocked the door to that cage of jealousy.

Now, I walk Free.

Always, the key is on the inside.

Time & Futility

It's painful.

Learning to dance their dance when among them.
Smiling a smile that's not really felt.
Being asked, and answering with words as empty
as the questions themselves...

At some point we stop.

Time and Futility make us the wiser,
as is their job to do.

We are not broken.
Just slow, sometimes.

Leave that kind of pain behind.
Show up and shine.

Find your people.

Search for those who can meet you
all the way in the center.

Whispers

Guilt imposes itself from the outside.
Its name is Shame. It sounds like "should."
It lies and it lies.
It says, "Letting me in
is easier than letting the truth, out."

Without a second thought, we jump on this train
of shame, of should, of self-sabotage.

Its only destination is the denial of self...
It keeps us from what we want to do and feel and be.

It is a loud and a dangerous fool,
persistent & insidious.
Dirty.

When ridden blindly, numbly, habitually,
Guilt serves only to abdicate integrity...
to keep us from
response-Ability.

Listen for the whisper.

The whisper waves and warns
with its little red flags.

Listen to the whisper.

The whisper points the way.

**validation
is for parking**

Moving On

"Moving on" for me, often feels like less of a choice
than a necessity...
consistently,
born of a truth not yet honored.

Clarity serves as midwifery,
a loud, screaming, messy, spastic fuckery.

"Moving on" includes a moving inward, simultaneously.
Encouragement can be helpful, but certainly,
it's not required for the birth
of what is meant to be.

In the name of practicing transparency,
so that you might see you,
by seeing me...

I have yet to "move on," gracefully.

Go

Become a student of longing, of wanting,
of things that don't even belong to you,
but maybe to someone else...
like your mother or father,
or their mother or father,
or theirs.

These are shadows...

Some feel mean.
Some carry sadness.
Some weep. Some beg.
Some are always wishing for something.
Most bring pain, so you notice.

They are determined that you see them.
They are masterful with their persistence.

Eaten alive by the consequences
of not paying attention to yourself, you cry.
You shake, you yell, you growl and fight.

In you go, haphazardly falling,
spiraling down the rabbit hole.

You have no power there, no control.

Open your doors to these shadows.
Don't slam them shut.
Invite them in.
Ask. Listen. Watch. Learn.

Open the door on you own accord.
You go first.
Step into the shadows with keen eyes,
consciously seeking the lesson,
the truth,
the purpose of their visit.

Open the door.

It can be dodgy in the shadows...
but that same message is always there.

The message is "Love."

Go.

vigilance
is the price
for freedom

Ancestors

Invite them into the darkest hours,
and ask them for guidance and light.

When grief stricken, drop the story
and listen for the echoes of their heartbreak,
bouncing off your own.

Express your gratitude fully and directly,
whenever you find yourself enjoying moments
of fortitude and strength.

Work toward breaking invisible chains,
by healing invisible wounds.

Ask for forgiveness
from the ancestors of those
that you bang up against,
in the simplest & ugliest of ways,
today.

Give back & push forward, all that's been received,
after cleaning it up with Love, the best you can.
Thrive on that.

Live the best, most beautiful
messy terrifying satisfying challenging life.
Survive *that*.

This is how we remember
& connect with
& honor
not only our ancestors,
but those we have created
and have not met,
yet.

Aho.

god bless
everyone we love
&
double god bless
everyone we don't love

It Hurts

There is no anesthetic for this.
It's hard to hold the handle,
while cutting at my own heart.

With my scream as my scalpel,
the sharpest & deepest of breaths
cannot reach the hell spot...

the This-Is-All-I-Got, spot.

There is an icy cold, numb, nugget
that is desperate to be opened
by my razor - raspy - primal - guttural
...howl.

How could you? God damn it.
How dare you come in here & ask me to betray myself,
after it took me so long just to get here?

No.

It cannot be reached.
It cannot be done.
To betray myself, is no longer an option.

And fuck -
It still hurts when you ask...

integrity
does not allow
intimacy
without safety

Light Interrupted

I lived in the dark for so long,
that when the lights finally came on,
I felt disoriented, frightened, and lost.

I tripped over things that seemed obvious to others.
I had to try things on for the first time, again & again,
until they became familiar.

Feeling around for something not yet known to me...

It called to me.
It haunted me.

As the darkness dissolved,
I was able to hear.

It was me.

- myself, my truth -
- my heart, my voice -

It was lonely in the light at first.
Exposing that...speaking it and sharing it
made it seem a little smaller.

It has been a worthy struggle
to admit myself to my Self,
and to god,
and to you.

Now shadows appear
when light is interrupted.

It is a reminder to come home...
to explore, to listen, to share, to shed,
to ask, to receive,
to honor,
to give

& to live...

in the light & in the dark
and in all the spaces,
in between.

there is always
more to the story
than could ever meet the eye

and we know the moment
it meets the heart
if it jives or
does not
jive

Let It Pour

There is always a season
to reflect, to feel,
to dig, to dissolve...
to fall apart,

so that we can be re-arranged.

Bring an umbrella and rainboots.
Bring a blanket and tea.

Above all else,
honor your truth.

And if the truth for you
is not merry & bright,
then don't be.

Let it pour.

WHICH PART

Stones

Each day
an old, dirty sack gets thrown over the back
and inside, the stones sit.

Like a nose or an ear,
there is a forgetting that it's there.

Resentments are cumbersome,
yet barely perceivable,
and somehow incredibly heavy.

Ask yourself. Ask.

What needs resolution?
What needs reconciliation?

Ask again. Ask some more.

Go in. Get clear.
Find a way to the heart of it.

Then stand up.
Stand up and move.

Reconcile.
Re-Solution.

Build something new, something exciting,
something that better speaks of Now...

Dunk that nasty sack
into the truth of this day, and this time.

And if the stones remain,
know why you have chosen to keep them...
Know how it serves you to carry them.
Know that you are choosing.

Be honest. Be brave.
Ask. Listen. Move.

Until yesterday is gone,
today is not real,
and tomorrow...the stones get heavier.

once I surrendered
I found a freedom I never would have known

if I hadn't been held captive
in the first place

Emotional Currency

Childhood wounds resurface to be acknowledged,
cellularly honored, and held up to the light...

They diligently demand perceptual accuracy,
to make space for emotional currency.

Then is not now. Now is not then.
This, we know in the head.

The heart, though,
can sense a bottomlessness
that feels chained to this life above ground.

That which stays
buried, hidden, denied...?
That thing festers. It grows.

Secrets feed on darkness.
They nip at awareness
&
annihilate instinctual needs
for safety and presence.

Find your people.
Dig, together.
Open. Unearth.
Shine some light.

Let the secrets know that you know.
You know that they exist.

Let them breathe.
Then let them go.

Keep moving gently forward.

The only way
to today.

Slay

It feels like I slay dragons every day.

I'm finding it does not serve
to run around
all pissed off
about that.

No

"No."

It's a very scary,
little two-letter word.

Without hands, it holds the key to freedom.

Without a long story to follow,
it leaves behind a trail of strength & knowing.

Kneed it into your being.

Let it resound automatically
when pressed upon by outside forces
that do not ring loudly
with your own personal truth.

The power of
"no"
creates & maintains
your integrity.

It will save your soul & it will hand you a life,
this wonderful, little
two-letter
word.

The Wolves

I know how to hold my wolves at bay,
so that you'll be comfortable,
so that I'll behave.

But some days?

I just don't fucking want to.

most things
are both things

make room
for all the things

Begin Again

I am astounded by how many times,
in a single day,
we can begin again.

We can start over.
We can wake up.

We can
Open.
Choose.
Love.
Give.
Receive.

Offer it up. Quiet it down.
Turn it around.

Birth something new.
Let go of something old.

Stop. Breathe.
Choose.

In a single day...

Die.
Come alive.

Be

...simply astounded.

Swing

I am done with the twiddle
of finding the middle,
of striving for balance,
and checking my valence.

I'm done with all the
TRY! TRY! TRY!
and always asking,
WHY? WHY? WHY?

The thing that really
satisfies,
is blowing kisses
at the center,
as I swing
wildly
by.

Within

Blind to our many gifts,
we look for life force,
as if it were somewhere outside of us.

We want experiences that will light the fire,
that will set the soul ablaze.

Being open to feel,
learning to discern, telling the truth,
making a conscious choice,
taking an honest action...

Now - there's a fire.

We are alive.

All that power, all that life force
is immediately, and experientially available.

On a simple whim,
we can go within.

the idea is not enough
the magic is in
the doing

Honor

Honor Your Truth. Apply action.
Don't just sit there. Do something.
Demonstrate.

Grateful?
Don't just say the words.
Do the thank you.

Grieving?
Write. Cry. Talk.
Scream. Wail. Walk.

Proud?
Sing it. Show it.
Throw your shoulders back.
Chin up. Chest out. Cheer.

Angry?
Break something. Make something.
Get it out. Growl. Howl. Run.

Bored?
Stomp. Bitch. Moan.
Pout. Grumble. Complain.

Honor your boredom
by loudly rolling around in it - literally.

I promise a great reward, if but a simple giggle
at your out loud, silly, wild, alive, human,
real, true, full, full
Self.

And if the doing
looks like stillness, and waiting,
and discerning, and deciding,
well then, honor the stillness
with consciousness, and intention...

knowing that you are giving
your whole entire Self
to the whole entire
experience.

Honor. Honor. Honor.

honor
is a verb

Absolutely

Give yourself the gift
of absolute generosity,
anywhere, at any time.

When we choose to remember
who and what we really are...

when we
choose to connect...

we will be met.

Generously.
Absolutely.

Every. Single. Time.

Allow It

sit and watch
and wait

and
place
each thought
in a bag
until

there is
nothing
but
stillness

watch - wait

wait - watch

the body
dissolves

what is left

allow it
to be loved

Arranging Furniture

Did I jump? Was I pushed?

Or was I pushed because
I said I wanted to jump?

Either way,
I'm falling now.

Not in a flailing, freaky,
free fall kind of way...

more like,
oozing through
a slightly see-through plasma,
surrounded by particles of...

next right things
to do.

It can be tricky to arrange
just a few pieces of furniture
in such a large space, though.

Don't you think?

living
the Tao

belonging
nowhere

I am
at home
everywhere

Inside Out

Life feels lighter when being led
from the inside out,
rather than from the top down.

Those we love notice
when jaws and hearts
unclench.

From here,
there is nothing to climb over,
to fight through or suffer from.

Torment comes
from the silly,
insufferable, mind.

The heart doesn't choose busy.

The heart prefers
presence and peace,
love and creation,
connection and kindness.

It is from this place,
from the inside out,
that we soften.

Soften often.

Give yourself permission
to move gently forward...
open, aware, curious.

if I only had a moment to tell you
the most important thing...

it would be that you
are so very
loved

In Further

With my heart open wide, and my eyes closed tight,
I stare into the darkness with anticipation and delight.
I listen to the silence with reverence,
with vigilance & curiosity...

Once I have settled into my seat,
in a room that I have created,
inside my very own castle,
my highest self walks in.

Finally,
I meet the version of me
that I have come here to be.

Good god, she is beautiful.
She is shiny and confident,
peaceful and whole.

I am shown with dancing colors, and I am told without words.
There's a swirling & a rising & a fading.
Colors & light & atoms are bouncing.
I hear popping & smashing & laughing.
It is expansion and movement, bubbles, and joy.

It is not from the outside, in.
It is from the inside, in further.

It is for me, of me, by me...
And simultaneously,
it is impersonal and eternal.

I open to it, dive in, swim around, breathing it in...
It is Love. I allow it to engulf me.
Completely.

I desire to hold it, but don't.
I let it all go.

I open my heart,
and close my eyes.

I stare into the darkness,
with anticipation and delight.

LAST PART

Silly

When there is the time & space to do Nothing,
so much Something is happening.

While doing the Nothing,
Anything and Everything
seems possible.

Isn't that
the silliest thing?

Truth & Tea

Desirous, disturbed, pensive, perturbed
- about to engage in self-sabotage -
I go ahead & have tea with my shadow.

After some talk, some time, and some quiet,
the truth comes out, as it always does.

Apparently, I am afraid of my own power.

There is a quiet knowing
that if I fully honor
the inside and the outside
of my entire being...

I will know what I am capable of.
I will know my purpose for being here.

The question remains.

"Why am I so afraid of becoming Love?"

Humility

micro macro cosm cosm
macro micro cosm cosm

Who really knows their right size
at any given time?

Humility requires
the courage and willingness
to practice flexible perspective.

It doesn't have to be taken so seriously.

Go and have yourself a giggle
as you move from big to little.

All of that morphing and
switch back and forthing
can become an actual joy ride.

Hop on. Hold on.

The switch is on the inside.

I am my mother
in so many ways

I miss her and wish
I could tell her

Unfurl

When there is no
clear sight
and only a
muddled
crashing
of words,

how well
does it work to
react
or
respond?

I, personally,
will wait...

My own experience
informs me of flowers
that unfurl beautifully

in their own
time.

balance
the universe will always come into
balance

what a wise
&
beautiful teacher

Unzippable Skins

Last night
I sat
for the magic
I showed up
for myself
I went in

I went in
past the layers
like unzippable
skins

There were
so many
to cut
through

Like metal
Like iron
Like chains

They dropped
to the floor
in a pile
by my shins

Like wood
Like bark
Like skin
I went in

They got lighter
Like leaves
Like paper
Like feathers

They dropped
They floated
They wafted
They slid

Then there was
air but thick
Like palpable
Like wind

Then cool
Then warmth
Then water
Then light

Then a clear
sort of jello
a prism - like
rainbow

Just movement
and rhythm
and flow

Like strength
Like presence
Like calm

Saying
Stop it
Drop it
It's not yours
to carry

It's small
It doesn't matter
It's not
the right size

You are bigger
You are magic
You are here
You are needed

To see
&
To be
What you really are

Which is
This
Here

Now

Sublime

There is something so sublime about sinking into Self...

In

...to grounded strength, known resilience, rooted perspective.

There is a freedom, a grace.
There is wonder and peace.

There is a curious sort of folly here.

I think I'll stay for a while,
as this is where I know

what is and is not
mine.

The Need

There are days when truth telling

is

hard and uncomfortable, yet

so

very, very necessary

that

"hard" & "uncomfortable"

become bullshit words

when compared to

our need

to live

in the light.

none of us will be free
until all of us are

Well – Worn

All you have suffered
and all you've endured

all that you've hidden from
and then finally faced

all that you've walked through
alone and with help

all that you've healed through
&
integrated and applied

all the crazy,
broken - scattered - shattered
pieces of it

become the well-worn tools
that you will use

to serve
others.

Perspective

Who has enough perspective to judge another?

Who can see the eternity of your soul, and its path,
or where you are, on that path, exactly?

And if someone did have that kind of vision,
I believe there would be no judgement.

Only love.

For to know your travels, your pain,
the efforts you've made in plain survival,
in emotional growth & spiritual evolution

through the ages...

To know your attempts, successes, failures, and heartbreaks
in being hopeful, courageous, and kind...
in having faith and maintaining integrity...
in knowing humility and making amends...

To know your expressions of
pure gratitude and joy and sadness...
To know those things about anyone
would be to know only love.

No judgement.

I Am You

I'm a person
I am stories
I am hopeful
I am bold

I laugh, I cry
I fail, I try
I am young
and I am old

I am
everything & nothing

I am
particles & light

I am breathing, I am here
I am day & I am night

I am all the colors
I am very single hue

I am humble
I am gorgeous

I am me

&

I am you

I Am New

I am new at being older...

heavier in some ways
and lighter in others

quicker in seeing and
slower in speaking

kinder to self
for sure

reminiscent & grateful
more than
resenting or lamenting
what is gone

wiser

less wanting
more giving

braver

prone to flying
when fully grounded
to places I've only dreamt of before

places of
acceptance & self-love & discipline
of knowing & letting go
of resting & taking in

places of
being & breathing
in rhythms I notice
and
care for & treasure

I am new
at being older

and I like it.

Goals

My life
is the life
I would want to live
if it wasn't
already mine.

I am
who I
would want to be
if I wasn't
already me.

Infinity Broken

eternal soul interrupted
by a short life on this tiny planet

one choice followed by a bazillion more before
we are interrupted & reconnected

feelings
thoughts
behaviors
agreements
broken & honored
entered into
again & again
hopefully

yearning
leaning
learning
growing
in love
integrity, gratitude, truth
until

a going home
a reconvening
a dancing among the particles

a celebration
a recalibration
a reconfiguration of
Ourselves as
Everything
Nothing
&
All Else

and then we start
all over
again

Infinity
Broken

...and not

Risk

The problem is, we think we have time.
Why wait? Wait for what? Wait for how long?

You've already lived through
what another part of you
still needs to hear...

Life lessons
True stories
Tales of becoming

Real.

Search your own cabinets for
courage, willingness, integrity.
They are there.
Reach in.

Risk.
Risk.
Risk.

Risk your whole entire self

Every. Single. Time.

I dare you....

Dear Past Self

I see you.
I hear your cry.
And even though no one else
is saying it to you right now,
you are so very
loved.

I know who you will become.
You will become who I am now
because buried deep inside of you
are seeds of strength and
courage and resilience.

You will keep on getting up.
You will keep on seeking.
You will keep on trying.

I cheer for you.
I send you love.
I often wish
I could actually
hold you in my arms.

I have carved you a path
and left signposts
along the way.

Honor the whispers.
Heed the red flags.
I promise you can trust them all.

Keep Moving Gently Forward.

Where we are now
is worth every single bit
of the fight and the rage,
the confusion, frustration and, fear...
every embarrassment, every heartbreak
and every one of you tears.

Keep coming.
I am you.

I am here.

Dig

May your well
Be deep
And clean
And airy
And light
And full.

And if it's not,
Open.

Start digging.

no more autopilot
go inside
learn to fly

CPSIA information can be obtained
at www.ICGtesting.com
Printed in the USA
LVHW020526260122
709443LV00010B/993